PLAYS FOR PERFORMANCE

*A series designed for
contemporary production and study
Edited by
Nicholas Rudall and Bernard Sahlins*

EURIPIDES

Iphigenia in Aulis

In a New Translation by
Nicholas Rudall

Ivan R. Dee
CHICAGO

Library of Congress Cataloging-in-Publication Data:
Euripides.
    [Iphigenia in Aulis. English]
    Iphigenia in Aulis / Euripides ; in a new translation by Nicholas Rudall.
       p. cm. — (Plays for performance)
    ISBN 1-56663-112-2 (cloth : alk. paper). — ISBN 1-56663-111-4 (pbk. : alk. paper)
    1. Iphigenia (Greek mythology)—Drama. I. Rudall, Nicholas. II. Title. III. Series.
PA3975.I7R83   1997
882'.01—dc21   97-14818

INTRODUCTION

by Nicholas Rudall

Euripides wrote *Iphigenia in Aulis* shortly before his death in 406 B.C. and a few months before Athens was defeated by Sparta in the Peloponnesian War. *Iphigenia Among the Taurians* was written about ten years earlier. The chronology of events in the two plays is therefore the reverse of their composition. If the plays are to be performed together, it would seem better to ignore the dates of composition and opt for the natural sequence of the story.

Both plays have as a central theme the horror of human sacrifice. In many ways this pivotal fact has been marginalized by literally centuries of scholarship. Human sacrifice was accepted as a "given" element of the myth, an occasion that afforded the possibility of conflict between Agamemnon and Clytemnestra. Recent scholarship has given this central theme more weight, even allowing that it may represent a vestigial memory of actual sacrifice. (The same argument is now acceptably applied to the story of Abraham and Isaac.) It would be a mistake for any contemporary production to ignore the central horror and relegate the issue to merely the given elements of the myth.

The story of the sacrifice of Iphigenia is not to be found in Homer, but secondary sources suggest that Hesiod told of her rescue by Artemis. In any case, her story is a part of the saga of the Fall of the

House of Atreus and a frequent subject of fifth-century drama. The chorus of Old Men in Aeschylus's *Oresteia* sings of her sacrifice at the hands of Agamemnon. In Sophocles' *Electra* her death is Clytemnestra's defense for her treatment of Electra and Orestes—as it is in Euripides' version of the play. All in all, her story forms a vital part of the moral dilemmas posed in many extant (and lost) plays.

What strikes our modern sensibility as particularly strange is the number of *different* versions of the story. We are used to single versions of our myths (Abraham and Isaac). Not so for the Greeks of the ancient world. Roberto Calasso, in his provocative and brilliant book *The Marriage of Cadmus and Harmony*, suggests that the retelling and reshaping of the individual stories was central to the prismatic way the Greeks viewed their religious and cultural myths. In other words, whereas we gravitate toward a single version of a story, finding its truth in its uniqueness, the Greeks believed that "truth" could be found only through multiple prisms. This tendency is especially apparent in the *Iphigenia* plays of Euripides. Not only do the two plays present radically different versions of the events, but their own endings suggest that the gods have yet other alternatives. Unfortunately the endings of both plays are corrupt and irredeemably lost, but this affords a modern production the license to rearrange and invent.

These translations are meant for the stage. As with all other plays in this series, the language is meant to be spoken. Euripides presents a curious challenge to the modern translator. His style is not to be captured by a single tone. Achilles speaks quite differently from Agamemnon, Clytemnestra from Iphigenia. *Iphigenia in Aulis* takes place just be-

4

fore the sacrifice. Clytemnestra and Iphigenia have been summoned by Agamemnon on the pretext of a marriage between Achilles and Iphigenia. Remember that this play was written as the Greek world was finally imploding at the end of the Peloponnesian War. We meet Menelaus and Agamemnon—not the mighty heroes of the Trojan War but two venal and callous contemporary generals. They pay lip service to the honor of the sacrifice. In the end the young and the innocent will die so that the war may go on. And their speech patterns are often rough and contemporary, venal and callous too. Achilles, on the other hand, speaks with the gallantry and even the arrogance and pomposity of a knight in armor.

There is humor in these plays. The old man servant at Aulis is a grumpy and hard-nosed fellow, almost reminiscent of the slaves in comedy. *Iphigenia Among the Taurians* has many situations which if not truly comic nevertheless are intentionally amusing. Both plays are remarkably theatrical. The twists and turns of the plots are filled with suspense. Catastrophe is ever imminent. Ultimately it is survived. But the audience is made to face the unthinkable— murder in the shape of human sacrifice.

CHARACTERS

AGAMEMNON, father of Iphigenia, husband of
  Clytemnestra, king of Mycenae
MENELAUS, brother of Agamemnon, husband of
  Helen
CLYTEMNESTRA, mother of Iphigenia, wife of
  Agamemnon
IPHIGENIA, daughter of Agamemnon and
  Clytemnestra
ACHILLES, son of Peleus
CHORUS
OLD MAN
MESSENGERS

Iphigenia in Aulis

Agamemnon's tent

AGAMEMNON: Hey! Old man! Come over here. To my tent.

OLD MAN: I'm coming. Agamemnon, my lord, what is on your mind, sir?

AGAMEMNON: Do you want to know? Then . . .

OLD MAN: I'm coming. I'm coming. I am old, but my mind is clear, my eyes are sharp.

AGAMEMNON: What star is that in the sky?

OLD MAN: Sirius. It shines there in the center of the heavens, following hard behind the seven Pleiades.

AGAMEMNON: The birds are silent. The sea is silent. And the winds are at peace on the banks of the Euripus.

OLD MAN: But, my lord, why are you pacing back and forth before your tent? Yes, there is calm here in Aulis. The guards on the walls are still. Let us go inside.

AGAMEMNON: I envy you, old man. I envy a man who lives a life without a name. But those that have power—I envy them least of all.

OLD MAN: But such men have a life of glory.

AGAMEMNON: A glory that is filled with danger. Yes, power is sweet, but it stands on the brink of grief. Sometimes it is the gods who destroy a man's life.

11

Sometimes it is the minds of men, vicious and beyond number, that bring ruin.

OLD MAN: These thoughts do not belong to a king. You are the son of Atreus. Pure happiness is your birthright. Your fate is to live in both joy and pain. You are human. Mortal. And whether you like it or not, the gods' will will be done. But you've been writing a letter, haven't you? You wrote it by lamplight. And you have it in your hand. Yes. You've been writing the same words over and over again. You read it, you tear it open, then you throw the lamp to the ground. And the tears! Streaming down your cheeks! You are behaving like a man out of his mind. Tell me of your pain, my lord. What has happened? My king, speak to me. Share your grief. I am a good man, loyal. I was a part of your wife's dowry. I was picked by Tyndareus because I was honest. Speak to me.

AGAMEMNON: Leda had three daughters—Phoebe, my wife Clytemnestra, and Helen. It was for her, Helen, that the richest young men in Greece came as suitors. And they fought violently against each other. Threats of murder were commonplace. If a man seemed likely to win her he would be killed. Helen's father faced a dilemma. Should he give her away or not? Her fate, their fate, was in the balance. Then he had an idea. He would require, on oath, each suitor to make a compact, one with the other, that whoever won Helen as his wife would be protected by all the other suitors. They sealed this oath with a burnt offering. Further, if any man should take her from her home and husband, they *all* should turn upon that man, make war and sack and level his city, Greek or barbarian. The suitors swore, but her father tricked

[handwritten margin notes: "exposition" with arrow circling "my wife Clytemnestra"; "her beauty a danger"]

them. He gave his daughter permission to choose the suitor whom her heart had kissed with the sweet breath of love. She chose Menelaus. Would to god she had not.

From Troy to Sparta came Paris. Paris, the judge of beauty, the judge of the beauty of goddesses. He came in gold and flowered beauty, barbarian opulence. He fell in love with her, she with him. Menelaus was away. Paris stole her, raped her, took her to Troy to Mount Ida, rich in cattle. Menelaus fell into a fury. He ransacked Greece for the rejected suitors. He made all Greece stand by the oath that the young men had sworn. Vengeance. The Greeks took up arms. And now we are here at Aulis, by the narrows of the sea. We have ships and shields, chariots and horses. Menelaus is my brother. That is why I am commander-in-chief. The people's choice. Would to god another had been chosen.

When we were all here, poised to set sail and fight, the winds died. We could not move. We were in despair. The prophet Calchas addressed the army. He said that my daughter, Iphigenia, must be sacrificed to Artemis, the goddess of this place. If she were sacrificed, we would be free to sail and take the land of Troy. If she were not sacrificed, we would not sail and Troy would stand. When I heard him speak I ordered our herald Talthybius to dismiss the assembly. I could not kill my own daughter. But my brother savaged me with arguments and persuaded me to commit the unspeakable! It was then that I wrote a letter, folded it, attached my seal, and sent it to my wife. In it I asked her to send my daughter here. She would be married to Achilles, I said. I praised the man, told her that he would not sail to Troy unless he had a bride from our family to take home

13

with him. It was a trick. I had to deceive my wife. The marriage is a trick. Of the Greeks, only Calchas, Odysseus, and Menelaus know.

This was wrong! What I did was wrong. But this time I have written the truth. That is why you saw me in the dark, tearing and sealing, sealing and tearing. Take this letter. Go to Argos. What I have written here I will share with you. You are a friend of mine and of my wife and of my house.

OLD MAN: Yes, tell me. Explain. When I speak to them, the words should ring true on my tongue.

AGAMEMNON: Daughter of Leda, Clytemnestra, this letter will bring you a new message. Do not send your daughter to Aulis, wreathed in calm. We must wait for another time to celebrate our daughter's marriage.

OLD MAN: But what about Achilles! When he loses his bride, won't his heart burst in anger? Anger against you and your wife? There is great danger here. Explain. Talk to me.

AGAMEMNON: There *is* no marriage. It is but a fiction. Achilles knows nothing. Nothing of the marriage. Nothing of the plan. He does not expect to hold my daughter in his arms.

OLD MAN: To bring her here, not as a bride promised to the son of the goddess, but as a victim to be slaughtered for the Greeks! This was an act of darkness.

AGAMEMNON: I was out of my mind. I had fallen into the dark path of madness. Now you must go— and quickly. Conquer your old age.

OLD MAN: My king, I leave in haste.

AGAMEMNON: Do not rest by cooling springs. Do not give in to sleep.

OLD MAN: No, my lord, no.

AGAMEMNON: When you come to the fork in the road, look about you. Make sure that my daughter's carriage does not fly past you. She must not come here to the Greek ships.

OLD MAN: I will see to it.

AGAMEMNON: And if you cross their path as they race from the safety of the palace, turn them back. Seize the reins, send them back to the altars of Argos.

OLD MAN: But when I speak to them, why should your wife and daughter trust me?

AGAMEMNON: Take this ring. It bears the same seal as the letter. Now go. See, dawn is already bringing her light. The sky brightens with the fire of the chariot of the Sun. *(Old Man leaves)* Bring me freedom from my troubles. No man can be counted happy until the end. No. We are all born into pain.

CHORUS: We have come to the sea-washed sands of Aulis.
We have left our home, the city of Chalcis, wrapped in the arms of the sea, nurse of the sweet spring water of Arethusa, and sailed through the waters of Euripus.
We have come to see the army of the Greeks
And the seafaring ships of the Greeks—the demigods.
Our husbands told us that golden-haired Menelaus and Agamemnon, the great king, had sent them to bring back Helen,

15

Sent them in a thousand ships of pine.
Paris, the shepherd, had carried her off from the
   rushy banks of the Eurotas.
Helen, a gift to Paris from Aphrodite when she
   emerged from her bath of dew and won the
   judgment of beauty over Hera and Athena.

I came in haste through the grove of Artemis,
The grove where many a victim has died.
I ran, my cheeks blushing with shame.
For I longed to see the Greeks, the demigods,
   their shields and weapons glinting in the sun.
Yes, and the great army of horsemen.
I gazed in wonder.
Sitting together were those two heroes who each
   bear the name Ajax.
The son of Oileus and the son of Telamon, glory
   of Salamis.
They were playing at drafts, taking pleasure in
   strategy and deceit.
There was Merion, son of Ares, for whom mortal
   men feel awe.
There Odysseus,
There Nereus, most beautiful of all the Greeks.

I saw Achilles racing like the wind.
Achilles whom Thetis bore,
Whom the centaur Chiron steeled into
   manhood.
I saw Achilles there on the sands, in full armor,
   racing on the shore.
He raced against a four-horse chariot,
Rounding the course,
Racing to victory.
Eumelus the charioteer screamed in fury.
I saw his glorious horses
With bits of gold and harness of gold.
Eumelus whipped them hard,

Whipped their gray dappled backs, their manes
    flecked with white.
These were the yoke horses.
The trace horses were bays with mottled fetlocks,
And I saw them, I saw them as they grazed the
    post at the course's end.
And always beside them raced Achilles.
There by the chariot rail.
There by the spinning wheels.
And always beside them raced Achilles.

I turned my gaze upon the ships.
Anchored in the thousands, they thrilled my
    woman's heart.
Oh a sight as sweet as liquid honey!
Fifty swift ships commanded by Achilles lay in the
    sun,
Sterns of gold glinting with the image of his
    goddess mother.

And there the Argive fleet
There the sixty ships of Athens commanded by
    Hippolytus.
Athena too shone on a winged horse of gold,
And the hearts of the sailors sang with pride.
The ships of Boeotia!
Cadmus at the helm and a dragon of gold beside
    him.
Ships from Phocis, ships from Locris,
Ships too from glorious Mycenae
Where Agamemnon is a mighty king.
In vengeance has he come to bring home the
    woman
Who sought an alien and barbarian bed.
There too the ships of Pylos,
Old Nestor at the helm and a bull of gold beside
    him.
Ships from Aenis, ships from Elis,

17

Ships from Taphos and from Salamis,
Ajax at the helm.
All, all arrayed before my eyes
All, all imprinted in my woman's heart.
Ah, this is a fleet that will crush its enemies!

And yet I hold locked in my mind what I have
heard at home.

(enter Old Man and Menelaus, quarreling)

OLD MAN: This is an outrage! My lord! This is not
right!

MENELAUS: Keep away from me! You are too loyal to
your master.

OLD MAN: Sir, I am honored by your reproach.

MENELAUS: You'll be sorry if you go too far.

OLD MAN: It is you who have gone too far. You have
opened the letter I was carrying.

MENELAUS: You were carrying the destruction of the
Greeks.

OLD MAN: Argue your point with someone else. Give
me back the letter.

MENELAUS: No! Let go!

OLD MAN: Never! Give it back!

MENELAUS: I shall hit you on the head with my scepter.

OLD MAN: To die for one's master is a glorious death.

MENELAUS: You talk too much for a slave. Let go!

OLD MAN: Agamemnon! My Lord! We are being at-
tacked!

(enter Agamemnon)

OLD MAN: He has taken the letter! By force! Justice means nothing to him.

AGAMEMNON: What is going on here? What is the meaning of this?

MENELAUS: First listen to *me*. I have the greater right to speak.

AGAMEMNON: Menelaus, my brother, why are you quarreling with this man? Why the violence?

MENELAUS: Look me in the eyes before I begin. That is all the proof I will need.

AGAMEMNON: I am the son of Atreus who feared nothing. Shall I be afraid to look you in the eye?

MENELAUS: You see this letter? This messenger of death?

AGAMEMNON: I see it. Give it to me.

MENELAUS: The Greeks shall first know all that is in it.

AGAMEMNON: So, you have broken the seal and read it. It was not for your eyes.

MENELAUS: Yes, I read it. I know your secrets and your shame. You will regret it.

AGAMEMNON: Gods above! The arrogance of the man! Where did you waylay my messenger?

MENELAUS: I was waiting for your daughter to come here from Argos.

AGAMEMNON: Why?

MENELAUS: Because I felt like it. I am not your slave.

AGAMEMNON: This is an outrage. Am I not to be master of my own house?

MENELAUS: Not when you are a cheat and a liar, when you slither your way into everything.

AGAMEMNON: You talk to me of cheating and of lying. You! I hate a facile, quick tongue.

MENELAUS: And I hate a devious, quick mind. You know neither justice nor honesty. I will prove your guilt. No lies, my brother! No quick denials. You cannot bluff your way out of this. Listen to me. I will not be too hard on you. Do you remember your past ambitions? To be leader of the Greeks against Troy? You pretended to be reluctant. But in your heart you longed for it. And to get it you groveled. You shook everyone by the hand. Your doors were open to all who wished to enter. You spoke to everyone, whether they wanted to listen or not. You were nice to everyone. You wanted to be popular. You wanted no rivals. But then when you were made commander-in-chief, you changed your tune. You abandoned all your old friends. You were inaccessible. You locked your doors. You rarely appeared in public. Brother, a good man does not change when he gets on in the world.

That is precisely the time when his friends ought to be able to count on him, when his power and success allow him to do more for them than ever. This is my first point, my first reproach—your lack of character. Then, when the Greek army came here to Aulis and we were denied a favoring wind, you became the lowest of the low. This injunction of the gods filled you with fear. The Greeks shouted at you, demanded that the fleet turn back, that you put an end to this futile delay. One could see the distress on your face. You could not bear the thought of not launching your thousand ships, of not filling the fields of Troy with the cries of war. So you came to me. "What shall I do? How can I get out of this?" You were afraid of losing your command, losing the glory.

Then Calchas spoke. You were to sacrifice your daughter. Only then would the Greeks be free to sail to Troy. You were quick to make promises. And your heart smiled. No one forced you to do what you did next. You cannot say that. You sent word to your wife that your daughter was to come to Aulis and be married to Achilles. That was the pretext you devised.

And now? You have been caught red-handed. You have changed your mind and sent a different message. You are no longer prepared to be your daughter's killer. I cannot be more blunt. This is the same heaven that bore witness to your oaths. Think! You are not unique. Many a man has worked hard to gain power. And many a man has lost that power in shame. Sometimes it is the fault of the people. They do not understand the complexity of power. But just as often it is the man himself who is incompetent and fails to protect the interests of the people.

My tears are for Greece. She planned an action steeped in glory. Now she must suffer the mockery of barbarians. All because of you and your daughter. It is not courage that makes a great leader or a great general. It is intelligence. A man who has half a brain can be governor of a state. But a commander-in-chief must be blessed with intelligence.

CHORUS: When brothers fight and anger and recrimination fly between them, there is only sorrow.

AGAMEMNON: Now it is my turn to criticize you. I will be compassionate, not arrogant. I will show you

21

the respect due a brother. Compassion springs from a good heart.

Tell me first why you are so angry. You are short of breath, your face is flushed. Why? Who has done you wrong? What do you want? Do you desire to win yourself a good wife? I cannot help you there. You had no control over the one you had. *You* made the mistakes. Must *I* pay for them? *I* do not have an adulteress for a wife. You talk of my ambition. But it is not *that* which torments you. No. You long to hold a beautiful woman in your arms. Discretion and common decency mean nothing to you. Your passions make you grovel. You have become an evil man. If I have the intelligence to undo a previous mistake—am I to be called a fool? You are the fool. You lost a faithless wife and now you want her back—be the gods willing.

Think back. The suitors who pursued Helen swore all manner of oaths to her father. But *you* won her hand. Not through strength or virtue but by the help of a goddess—the goddess of Hope. You want an army? Conscript the suitors! Be their general! They were fools before, why not now?

But the gods are not fools. They know when an oath has been sworn under duress and when a promise is evil. I will not kill my child.

Why should you, with no concern for what is right, take vengeance on a worthless wife and live a life of happiness and success while I am forced to weep unending tears for my sins, my unjust unconscionable sins against my own child?

I shall say no more. I have been brief and to the point. If you will not see sense, that is your choice. But I must follow my conscience and do what I must do.

CHORUS: Your words have changed—for the better. You now refuse to harm your child.

MENELAUS: Then I am alone. I have no friends.

AGAMEMNON: Not true. Simply stop destroying the friends that you have.

MENELAUS: Are you our father's son!? Prove it!

AGAMEMNON: We should be brothers in virtue, not in sin.

MENELAUS: If you *were* my friend, you would share in my misfortunes.

AGAMEMNON: Brother, you hurt me. If you chastise me, do it with some good in mind.

MENELAUS: Are you abandoning Greece in its pain?

AGAMEMNON: Greece, like you, is the victim of some god.

MENELAUS: Revel in the power of your crown. Betray your brother. I shall make new plans and other friends.

(enter Messenger)

MESSENGER: Lord Agamemnon, King of all the Greeks, I bring to you from your palace home your daughter Iphigenia, your noble queen Clytemnestra, and your son Orestes. Your queen knows that you will rejoice to see your son after your long absence from home.

The journey was long. Now the women are bathing their soft feet in the waters of a welcome stream. The horses are being watered and turned loose to browse upon the meadows' grass. I have come before, my lord, that you may have time to make ready. The army already knows—so quick is rumor—that your daughter has arrived. The men are running to see the entourage, to catch a glimpse of the girl. People in power, the rich, the famous, are always the objects of attention and speculation: "Is there to be a marriage? Did Agamemnon miss his family so much that he had her brought here?" And some are saying, "They are preparing bridal offerings to the goddess Artemis, Queen of Aulis. Who is to be the groom?"

Come then, my lord, begin the rituals. Fill the baskets, crown your head with flowers. Lord Menelaus, begin the marriage hymns, let the flutes echo in the halls and the sound of dancing feet ring in the air. This is a holy day that dawns for the princess.

AGAMEMNON: You have done well. Go into my tent. All will be well. What will be will be.

Aaah, what can I say, where shall I begin? The yoke of fate lies heavy on my neck. Yes, fate has outflanked me, has used a superior strategy in the field. Oh, to be born of humble stock has its rewards. Such men can weep and speak of their pain. But when a prince feels miseries like these he cannot weep. Decorum rules. And yet if I do not weep I shall feel deep shame. It is hard to be a king.

What shall I say to my wife? How shall I greet her, how look her in the eye? She has caught me off guard. I did not tell her to come. I had troubles enough before. But I should have known she would not let her daughter come alone. She wanted to be the mother of the bride, perform the rituals, surrender her precious dau— Oh God the pain—! She will uncover my sin. Oh my poor virgin daughter—why use that word?—she

24

will soon be the bride of death! Aaah, I can see her now on her knees, begging me, "Father, will you kill me? I pray that you and all your loved ones win such a marriage." Orestes will be there. Too young to speak, he will only whimper and weep. But all will understand his infant cries. Aaah, my curse on you Paris, son of Priam. You have destroyed me. When you stole Helen, you stole my life.

CHORUS: I am moved by pity. We are strangers, but we weep for the grief of the king.

MENELAUS: Brother, give me your hand.

AGAMEMNON: I give it. Yours the victory, mine the sorrow.

MENELAUS: I swear an oath—I swear by Pelops, father of our father. I speak to you in plain and honest words. My heart is an open book.

When I see your tears I feel nothing but pity, and I weep too. I take back all my previous arguments. You have nothing to fear from me. Your way is the right way. Listen to my advice: do not kill your child, do not place any interests above your own. For you to groan in pain and me to smile in joy is no justice. Nor for your child to look on darkness, mine on light.

What is it I want? Marriage? There are other happier choices I can make. Should I bring ruin on my brother? What greater wrong could there be? Just to bring back Helen—a bad prize for a good? I was wrong, hotheaded. I did not stop to look closely at the problem. I did not see what it means to kill one's child. All I feel is compassion for the poor girl. To sacrifice her for the sake of my marriage! What has your daughter to do with Helen?

25

Dismiss the army. Let us leave Aulis. Weep no more, my brother, for you make me weep too. The oracles spoke to *you* about your daughter. To *me* they said nothing. My interests have become yours.

Why have I changed from anger and abuse? It is only natural. It is love, love for my own mother's son. That is why I have changed. And it is a change for the better. It is right for a man to seek the best solution to every problem.

CHORUS: You have spoken honorably, my lord— words fitting your noble descent from Tantalus, son of Zeus.

AGAMEMNON: I commend you, brother. I did not expect this. Your words are honorable and worthy of your place. When brothers quarrel it is often out of love or family rivalry. It is mutually painful. I hate it. But I must speak. Brother, I have no choice. Blood must be spilled. My daughter must die.

MENELAUS: Why? Who will force you to kill your own child?

AGAMEMNON: The Greek army.

MENELAUS: Not if you send her back to Argos.

AGAMEMNON: I could keep that a secret—but not the other thing.

MENELAUS: What other thing? Stand your ground before the mob.

AGAMEMNON: Calchas will reveal his oracles to the Greek army.

MENELAUS: Not if he dies first—and that is easy.

AGAMEMNON: The whole tribe of prophets is rotten with ambition.

MENELAUS: They are of no use—good or bad.

AGAMEMNON: One thing preys on my mind—are you afraid of it too?

MENELAUS: If you do not tell me, how can I answer?

AGAMEMNON: One man knows all about this—the seed of Sisyphus.

MENELAUS: Odysseus? Pah! We have nothing to fear from him.

AGAMEMNON: He is cunning—always manipulating the mob.

MENELAUS: Indeed he is ambition's slave—a deadly disease.

AGAMEMNON: Can't you see him now—standing in front of the Greek army, telling them about the prophesies of Calchas, telling them that I had sworn to make the sacrifice to Artemis but that I had gone back on my word? He will win the army over, incite them to kill us both first and then sacrifice the girl. Even if I escape to Argos they will come after me, destroy our ancient walls, and raze the city to the ground. This is my burden and my grief. There is nothing I can do. I am the plaything of the gods. Do one thing for me, my brother: when you go amongst the men, say nothing and make sure that Clytemnestra hears not a word of this—until I have taken my child and offered her to the god of Death. I have a deed to do of deepest woe. Let me do it with as few tears as possible.

Women, keep silence.

CHORUS: Blessed are they who share the fair
   happiness of marriage.
Blessed are they whom Aphrodite rules with
      gentleness,
Who live a life of peace free from passion's
   torment.
Golden-haired Eros takes aim with a double bow.
One wound brings happiness,
The other, life's undoing.
Oh sweet Aphrodite,
Keep love's deep wound far from my
   bedchamber.
Bless me with love's gentle grace.
Let me feel pure desires.
Oh come to me in due measure. Withhold your
   fury.

Mortal men have different natures, different
   customs.
True goodness shines clear.
Virtue thrives on nurture and good counsel.
True modesty is true wisdom.
Its beauty makes the mind see the right.
Virtue brings a fame that will not die.
Greatness lies in the pursuit of virtue.
Amongst women virtue must be a cloistered
   thing
When love calls.
Amongst men virtue takes many shapes.
It brings greatness to the cities of mankind.

Paris, upon Mount Ida, on the slopes which gave
   you life,
You drove your sleek white cattle.
On your pipes you played a barbarian melody,
The reeds breathed a sweet Olympian sound.
Then, as the fat cattle grazed, three goddesses
Came to judgment.

28

Hope stirred in your wild heart and you dreamed
  of Greece.
You stood before Helen's ivory palace.
She looked into your eyes.
Your eyes shot arrows of desire.
You were made mad by love.
War came, a war of ships and men,
War of Greece against the walls of Troy.

(enter Clytemnestra, Iphigenia, and Orestes with attendants)

CHORUS: Great is the blessedness of the mighty. Look upon Iphigenia, daughter of Agamemnon, princess of the people, and on Clytemnestra, Queen of Argos. The breed is noble. The fortunes high. In the eyes of mortals the powerful and wealthy are like gods.

Daughters of Chalcis, let us stand by and receive the queen as she steps from her carriage. With gentle hands give her firm support. And let not the glorious daughter of Agamemnon know fear when she comes among us. She is a stranger here, as are we.

CLYTEMNESTRA: You have greeted us with kindness and grace. I count that a good omen. For I hope that I come as the mother of a fortunate bride. Take from the carriage the gifts I have brought for my daughter's dowry. Carry them carefully into the house. Now, my child, step down and put your delicate feet upon the ground. You women, take her by the arms and help her down. One of you, give me your hand—that I may descend gracefully. You there, take the horse's reins. Their eyes grow wild and full of fear if none stand by to calm and soothe them. Take my son, Agamemnon's infant son, Orestes. My child, are you sleep-

29

ing? Did the carriage rock you to sleep? Wake up now and smile upon your sister's wedding day. My prince, you will have a fine new brother—Achilles, son of the Sea Nymph. Iphigenia, stand here by your mother. Show these strangers how happy and proud I am. Look, here comes your dear father. Go! Greet him!

IPHIGENIA: Don't be angry, mother. I must run to him—and hold my father in my arms.

CLYTEMNESTRA: King Agamemnon, most revered husband, we have come. We have obeyed your commands.

IPHIGENIA: I longed to see your face. Don't be angry.

CLYTEMNESTRA: Quite right, my child. You—of all my children—always loved your father the most.

IPHIGENIA: Father, I am so happy to see you. It has been so long.

AGAMEMNON: And I am happy to see you. You speak for us both.

IPHIGENIA: I give you my loving greetings. Thank you, father, for sending for me.

AGAMEMNON: Perhaps. Perhaps not, my child. I do not know.

IPHIGENIA: You look uncomfortable, father. You said you were happy to see me.

AGAMEMNON: There is much to think about—for a general and a king.

IPHIGENIA: Pay attention to *me* now. Forget your worries.

AGAMEMNON: I am with you, my child, all of me. My thoughts are only of you.
(irony)

IPHIGENIA: Then stop frowning. Smile, father, smile.

AGAMEMNON: I am as happy as I can be—just to see your face.

IPHIGENIA: But your eyes are filled with tears.

AGAMEMNON: We must be apart for an eternity.

IPHIGENIA: I do not understand. My dear father, I do not understand.

AGAMEMNON: You seem so self-assured, so sensible. It makes me weep all the more.

IPHIGENIA: Then I will talk nonsense. I want to see you laugh.

AGAMEMNON: *(aside)* Hell and damnation! I cannot hold my tongue. *(to her)* You are such a sweet child.

IPHIGENIA: Come home, father, come home and stay with us.

AGAMEMNON: Oh I want to! I weep because I cannot have what I want.

IPHIGENIA: Put an end to war! Forget the wrong done to Menelaus.

AGAMEMNON: I must put an end to other things first. And that is destroying me.

IPHIGENIA: You have been here in Aulis so long, hidden away.

AGAMEMNON: Yet even now there is something that prevents the army from sailing.

IPHIGENIA: Where is Troy, father?

AGAMEMNON: In a land where I would to god Paris did not live.

31

IPHIGENIA: You are going on a long journey, father, and leaving me behind.

AGAMEMNON: You too, my daughter, are going on a long journey.

IPHIGENIA: How I wish you could take me with you!

AGAMEMNON: When you set out on your journey, you will think of your father.

IPHIGENIA: Shall I journey alone or with my mother?

AGAMEMNON: Alone. You go where your mother and father cannot be with you.

IPHIGENIA: Have you found me a new home, father?

AGAMEMNON: Stop! It is not right for girls to ask such questions.

IPHIGENIA: When you have conquered Troy, come home to me quickly, father.

AGAMEMNON: Before I go I have to perform a sacrifice.

IPHIGENIA: I understand. The gods demand their holy rites.

AGAMEMNON: You will be there, my child. You will stand by the priests.

IPHIGENIA: Will there be dancing, father? Round the altar?

AGAMEMNON: *(aside)* How your innocence touches my heart. Go inside now. A young girl should not be seen in public. Take my hand. Kiss me. You are going a long way away from your home and from your father. Oh these soft cheeks! To hold you so close! Your golden hair! Helen and Troy have laid a heavy burden upon you. But I must stop. When

32

I hold you, tears flood my eyes. Go inside now. *(exit Iphigenia) (to Clytemnestra)* Daughter of Leda, forgive me if I seem to grieve too much over giving my daughter to Achilles. To part thus with one's child may be a thing of happiness, but it eats at a parent's heart too, when he gives away to another house the child he has raised with love and care.

CLYTEMNESTRA: I feel it too. Yes, I shall feel the same pangs when I lead my daughter forth when the marriage hymns are sung. No, I do not blame you. But marriage is a common thing and time dries all tears. I know the name of the bridegroom you have chosen, but I should like to know more about his family lineage.

AGAMEMNON: Aegina was the daughter of Asopus.

CLYTEMNESTRA: Married to a god or a mortal?

AGAMEMNON: To Zeus, who was the father of Aeacus, King of Oenone.

CLYTEMNESTRA: Which of his sons inherited the kingdom?

AGAMEMNON: Peleus—who then married a daughter of the god Nereus. (Thetis)

CLYTEMNESTRA: Given to him by the god or taken by force?

AGAMEMNON: Zeus sealed the contract, gave her in marriage. He was her guardian.

CLYTEMNESTRA: Where did he marry her? Beneath the waves her father ruled?

AGAMEMNON: No, at Pelion where Chiron lives.

CLYTEMNESTRA: Chiron and all the centaurs?

AGAMEMNON: Yes. There the gods celebrated the marriage of Peleus and Thetis.

CLYTEMNESTRA: And did she or her father bring up Achilles?

AGAMEMNON: Neither. Chiron did. So that he should grow up innocent of the wickedness of men.

CLYTEMNESTRA: Wise was the teacher. And wiser the man that gave him to the teacher.

AGAMEMNON: This is the man who will be your daughter's husband.

CLYTEMNESTRA: I can find no fault in him. Where in Greece does he live?

AGAMEMNON: In Phthia, on the banks of the Apidanus.

CLYTEMNESTRA: Will he take our daughter to live there?

AGAMEMNON: The one who possesses her will take care of that.

CLYTEMNESTRA: My blessings on them. When is the wedding day?

AGAMEMNON: At the full moon. That is a lucky time.

CLYTEMNESTRA: Have you begun the sacrifices to the gods? *ironic*

AGAMEMNON: I am about to do so. This duty consumes my mind.

CLYTEMNESTRA: And afterward—the marriage feast?

AGAMEMNON: Yes. When I have sacrificed to the gods the offerings they demand.

CLYTEMNESTRA: Where shall I hold the women's feast?

AGAMEMNON: Here, by the sleek Greek ships.

CLYTEMNESTRA: If that is your desire, it shall be so. May all be for the best.

AGAMEMNON: Wife! Do you understand what you are to do? You must do as I say!

CLYTEMNESTRA: I always do what you say.

AGAMEMNON: When the bridegroom comes I shall—

CLYTEMNESTRA: You shall what? Am I not to be here? It is a mother's right and duty—

AGAMEMNON: Here, amongst the Greeks, I shall give your child in marriage.

CLYTEMNESTRA: And in the meantime, where am I to be?

AGAMEMNON: Go back to Argos. Look after your other daughters.

CLYTEMNESTRA: And leave my child here? Who will raise the marriage torch?

AGAMEMNON: I shall provide the bridal torches.

CLYTEMNESTRA: That, sir, is not the custom. These are serious matters, not to be trifled with.

AGAMEMNON: It is not proper for you to mingle with the Greek soldiers.

CLYTEMNESTRA: It is not proper for a mother to be denied the right to give away her daughter.

AGAMEMNON: Your daughters should not be left at home alone.

CLYTEMNESTRA: They are well taken care of. They are safe in the women's quarters.

AGAMEMNON: Woman, obey me.

CLYTEMNESTRA: No, by Artemis, Queen of Argos! No. Go fight your wars abroad. These are domestic matters. They are mine to attend to.

(exit Clytemnestra)

AGAMEMNON: That was wasted labor. My plan to get my wife away from here did not work. I scheme and strategize against those I love best—and I am outmaneuvered and defeated. I must go to Calchas and together we will make arrangements for the god's pleasure—and for my pain. I carry the weight of Greece upon my shoulders. A wise man should keep a wife who is helpful and good—or else not keep one at all.

CHORUS: To Simois, to the swirling silvery waters,
    Will come the great army of the Greeks. Bristling
        with spears,
    To Troy will they sail, to the fields of Troy,
        Apollo's Troy,
    Where Cassandra wreathed in a garland of green
        laurel
    Tears the gold of her hair,
    And spasms of prophecy seize her limbs.
    So the story goes.

    The Trojans will stand on the battlements of
        Troy,
    Waiting for death.
    From across the sea, Ares with his shield of
        bronze, advances,
    Advances, with his sturdy ships, to the sea mouths
        of Simois.

Ares will bring back Helen, Helen the sister of
  Castor and Pollux,
Helen back to the Hellenes,
Troy destroyed. Greek spear and shield
  triumphant.

When Agamemnon has ringed the ramparts of
  Troy
And brought war's death to battlements of stone,
When he has cut the head of Paris from its neck,
Overturned the city, razed its walls,
Then will the women weep and Hecuba will
  mourn
And Helen will be washed with her own tears
And grieve for a husband lost.

I pray that never will such fear descend upon me
  or upon my children's children.
Fear falls heavy on the Trojan women rich in
  gold
As they sit and weave and sit and talk.
"What man will seize me by my soft rich hair
And pluck me, as a flower is plucked,
Take me in tears from my dying home?"
The sin is yours, Helen,
Daughter of the long-necked swan, so the story
  goes,
When Zeus became a white-winged bird.
So the story goes.
Or is it just a story, without truth or meaning?
A story for mankind but a poet's fancy merely.

(enter Achilles)

ACHILLES: Where can I find the general of the Greek
  army? Someone tell him that I, Achilles, son of
  Peleus, am at his door. We who spend our time
  waiting by the banks of the Euripus are not all
  alike. Some who sit here by the shore are unmar-

ried, some have wives and children, but all are seized by the same violent passion: The Greeks, perhaps by the gods' will, are obsessed with this expedition. Let me first state my own case. Others can speak for themselves. I left my father, Peleus, behind in Pharsalus. Here I wait for a breath of wind to stir the waters of Euripus. I am forced to keep my men, brave warriors of Myrmidon, under close constraint. They do not cease questioning me, pestering me—"Achilles, why are we waiting here? How long before we sail to Troy? Do something! If you are incapable, then take your army back home. Do not wait any more for the sons of Atreus who cannot make up their minds."

(enter Clytemnestra)

CLYTEMNESTRA: Son of divine Thetis, I overheard your words and came outside.

ACHILLES: To whom do I speak? A woman of grace and beauty. My respects, madam.

CLYTEMNESTRA: There is no reason why you should recognize me. We have not met before. You show me due respect. I thank you.

ACHILLES: Who are you? Why have you come here where the Greeks are gathered, a woman surrounded by armed men?

CLYTEMNESTRA: I am Clytemnestra, daughter of Leda, wife of Agamemnon.

ACHILLES: Your answer is short, madam, but clear. But it is not proper for me to talk so openly with a woman.

CLYTEMNESTRA: Stay. Do not run away. Take my right hand. Let us bless this happy marriage.

38

ACHILLES: Madam, I could not touch your hand. I could not face Agamemnon—I have no right to such intimacy.

CLYTEMNESTRA: What greater right do you need? You, son of Thetis, goddess of the sea, are to marry my daughter.

ACHILLES: Marry? What do you mean? I do not know what to say. You must be under some misapprehension.

CLYTEMNESTRA: You are shy. That is only natural when you meet your new family and marriage is mentioned.

ACHILLES: My lady, I have never wooed your daughter. Not a word has been said of marriage by the sons of Atreus.

CLYTEMNESTRA: What? Then you may well be surprised at my words to you. *I* am surprised at yours.

ACHILLES: Think, we must think. Together we cannot both be wrong.

CLYTEMNESTRA: *(to herself)* I have been tricked, dishonored. I have been matchmaking where there is no match. *(aloud)* Can this be true? I die of shame.

ACHILLES: Do not be distressed. Perhaps it is merely a joke played on us both. Pay it no mind.

CLYTEMNESTRA: Farewell, sir. I can no longer look you in the eye. I have been made a liar. I am humiliated. Farewell. *(she starts to leave)*

ACHILLES: Farewell to you. I shall go and find your husband here amongst the tents. *(he starts to leave)*

OLD MAN: *(from inside the tent)* Stay a moment, Achilles, stay! Yes, you, I mean, son of the goddess! And you too, daughter of Leda.

ACHILLES: Who is it that calls from behind these doors? He seems distressed. Who is it?

OLD MAN: A slave. No need to mince words. I am what I am. A slave.

ACHILLES: To whom do you belong? You're not one of mine. Agamemnon's?

OLD MAN: No, sir. I belong to the lady. Her father, Tyndareus, gave me to her.

ACHILLES: Come out here. I am not leaving. Why did you ask me to stay?

OLD MAN: Are you two alone, completely alone?

ACHILLES: There is no one. Speak. You can come out.

OLD MAN: *(enters)* May fate and my own prophetic power save those whom I want saved.

ACHILLES: You can make that speech at another time. It is a little heavy-handed, to say the least.

CLYTEMNESTRA: *(Old Man kneels)* You may touch my hand. What is it you have to say?

OLD MAN: You know me, madam. You know how devoted I've been to you and your children.

CLYTEMNESTRA: You have been with the family for a long time, yes.

OLD MAN: And you know that I was given to King Agamemnon as part of your dowry?

CLYTEMNESTRA: You came to Argos with me, yes. You have been my servant for a long time.

OLD MAN: So you can trust me. I am looking out for your interest. Your husband concerns me less.

CLYTEMNESTRA: Well? Tell me what you have to say.

OLD MAN: Your daughter is to die. Her father, her own father is going to kill her.

CLYTEMNESTRA: What are you saying? Silence! You are out of your mind!

OLD MAN: He will take his sharp sword and cut her white throat.

CLYTEMNESTRA: Has my husband gone mad? Oh sacred god!

OLD MAN: He is not mad. But where you and your daughter are concerned he has taken leave of his senses.

CLYTEMNESTRA: Why? Why? Why? What demon is driving him to do this?

OLD MAN: No demon but a prophecy, so Calchas says, if the army is to set sail.

CLYTEMNESTRA: Where? Oh my daughter! And what of me? To kill his own daughter! Sail where?

OLD MAN: To Troy, to bring back Helen.

CLYTEMNESTRA: For Helen's return must Iphigenia die?

OLD MAN: In a word, yes. Her father will sacrifice her to Artemis.

CLYTEMNESTRA: So. He pretended there was to be a marriage. And for a marriage *I* brought her here.

OLD MAN: Yes, you brought her here, in happiness, to be Achilles' bride.

CLYTEMNESTRA: Oh my daughter, you have come to meet your death, and I to ruin.

OLD MAN: You are both victims of an outrage beyond horror. What Agamemnon plans is savage butchery.

CLYTEMNESTRA: Oh there is nothing left, nothing. I can only weep, weep.

OLD MAN: Let the tears come. To lose a child is unendurable sorrow.

CLYTEMNESTRA: But how did you find this story out? Who told you?

OLD MAN: I was sent to you with a second letter.

CLYTEMNESTRA: Did the letter say *not* to bring my child, or like the first, command me to do so?

OLD MAN: It said not to bring her. At that moment he was sane.

CLYTEMNESTRA: Then, if you had such a letter, why did you not bring it to me?

OLD MAN: Menelaus stole it from me. He is the real cause of all this trouble.

CLYTEMNESTRA: Oh son of Thetis and Peleus, do you hear this!?

ACHILLES: I hear it. And I pity you. But some of this touches *me*. It cannot be ignored.

CLYTEMNESTRA: They will kill my child! Marriage to you was the bait in the trap. *(falls to her knees)* I beg you, here on my knees. I beg you. I am not ashamed. I am a mortal, you a goddess's son. I have no pride left in me. All I have is an obsession—for the safety of my child. Child of the goddess, take up my cause and hers, she that was to

42

be called your wife. Untrue, I know, but help her for all that. It was for you I brought her as a bride. But now it is for death that I have brought her. If you do not protect her, you will live in shame. You were not joined in marriage, but on people's lips you were the husband of my poor daughter. I beg you. I touch your right hand. I touch your beard. I touch your goddess mother's holy name. Your glorious reputation has been my ruin. Let it now protect me. I touch your knees in supplication. Your body is my altar. I have no friends to take my part. Agamemnon! Ha! You have heard of his hard heart and cruel mind. Look on me. I am a woman, a woman set amongst an army of sailors, sailors who know no laws, ready for anything. And yet, if they so choose, they can help our cause. If you will raise your hand in protection above our heads, we are saved. If you will not, we are lost.

CHORUS: To be a mother is to be possessed by a power beyond wonder. It lives in every mother's heart. For her child a mother will suffer any suffering.

ACHILLES: I am a proud man. My pride runs deep in my bones. But I have learned to temper my distress when there is trouble and my joy when there is success. That measure, that balance, is the mark of an intelligent human being. There are times when it is good not to think too much and to exercise good common sense. I was brought up in the house of Chiron. He was a man who feared the power of the gods. From him I learned to be direct. Where the sons of Atreus are concerned, if their leadership is good, I shall obey them. If it is not, I shall not obey. Here or in Troy

43

I shall be a free man. I am what I am. A soldier. My spear shall bring glory to the god of War.

The man who is closest to you, who should love you the most, has betrayed you. I offer you my compassion—all that a soldier can feel. Your daughter, who was called mine, will not be killed by her father. I am a man. I will not stand aside. Your husband will not play tricks with me. My name alone would be the killer of your child, a murderer which did not raise the sword. My body would be stained with pollution if this girl suffers horror beyond horror, outrage beyond outrage— if, in short, she must die because of the marriage, because of me.

They must think me the biggest coward in the army, a nobody. Menelaus is the great man. I am not the son of Peleus but the son of a scoundrel if I let my name be the death of your daughter. I swear by Nereus that lived in the sea, by Thetis that gave me birth, never shall King Agamemnon lay hands on your daughter. He shall not so much as touch her dress with his finger. I swear by Phthia, city of my birth—else call it not a city and bestow that name upon the savage village of Sipylus, home of the sons of Atreus.

And what of Calchas? He will pay dearly for his offerings of meal, his holy waters. What is a prophet? If he's lucky he gets one right out of ten. When his luck ends, so does he.

I do not say this to win a bride. Ten thousand would-be brides are hunting me down. King Agamemnon has insulted me. He used my name to entrap his child. He should have asked me. It was my name that made Queen Clytemnestra surrender her daughter. I would have *given* the Greeks the use of my name if it could have helped them sail to Troy. I would not have re-

dismisses a prophet -Achilles mistake

44

frained. In war I think deeply of the interests of my fellow soldiers. But now I am a nothing. My name is nothing. The generals do not care if they treat me well or ill. But my sword shall speak. It will be stained with the lifeblood of any man who tries to take your daughter from me. So rest easy. You see in me a god powerful enough to save you. If I am not one, I shall become one.

CHORUS: Son of Peleus, you have spoken, bringing honor to yourself and to your holy mother, goddess of the sea.

CLYTEMNESTRA: How can I not heap too much praise upon you, sir? *(aside)* And yet if I am too restrained I may lose his favor. When good men are praised they may feel uncomfortable with those that praise them—especially if the praise seems excessive.

I am ashamed, sir, that I have laid my private grief before you. My pain is not yours to suffer. But when a good man helps the weak, far removed though he be from their troubles, he becomes respected in people's eyes. Pity me. My sufferings deserve your pity. I thought when I arrived that you would be my daughter's husband, but I found that hope to be vain. Think now, if my daughter were to die, think of the curse that might bring upon a future marriage. That is not an idle warning. But your brave words, sir, ring like truth in my ears: if you so decide, my child shall not die. Should she fall upon her knees before you? If that would move you, sir, she shall kneel. A virgin should not have to behave so, but she shall come, eyes lowered, respectful. But if my prayers can win your heart, let her remain at home. She is shy. Perhaps too shy. We should do all we can to respect her modesty.

45

ACHILLES: Do not bring your daughter into my sight. No. Let us not give the vulgar occasion for sport. Soldiers, assembled from all over and free from the cares of home, love dirty gossip, love a bit of slander. But it does not matter to me whether you beg or no. My mind is made up. I must deliver you from danger. There is nothing more. Hear me and take heart. I will not tell a lie. If I were to deceive you in this, if I *were* to lie, then let me live no more. By my life, I shall save the girl.

CLYTEMNESTRA: May the gods bring you eternal blessing for helping the afflicted.

ACHILLES: Now we must act. Listen, so all may go well.

CLYTEMNESTRA: I am listening, sir.

ACHILLES: Let us persuade her father to change his mind.

CLYTEMNESTRA: He is a coward. He is afraid of the army.

ACHILLES: But there are arguments here that can win the day.

CLYTEMNESTRA: A slim hope. But tell me what I must do.

ACHILLES: Begin simply. Beg him not to kill the child. If you can persuade him, you will have no need of me. You and yours will be safe. If he denies you, then you must come to me. Persuasion is best. We could then all remain friends. And the army would support me if I use discretion, not force. If we succeed, all will be well and I will not be needed.

CLYTEMNESTRA: This is a wise beginning. I take your advice. But if this plan is not successful, where shall I find you? In my sorrow and in need of your protection, must I go looking for you?

ACHILLES: I shall be watching for you. I shall be near. You will not have to run around looking for me amongst the Greeks, angry and upset. Your honor will be protected and that of your ancestors. Tyndareus's name will be inviolate. It will ever be great amongst the Greeks.

CLYTEMNESTRA: So it shall be. I obey. I am your servant, sir. If there are gods, you will be blessed, for you are a man of virtue. If there are no gods, why should we suffer so?

CHORUS: What was the song that Hymenaeus, god of marriage, raised on his Libyan flute?
When the harp stirred the dance and the pipes sang in the air,
When the Muses of the golden hair came from Mount Paulina
Down to the feast of the gods,
When they beat the earth with their sandals of gold?
To the marriage of Peleus they came.
In the valleys of the centaurs,
In the woodlands of Mount Paulina,
Sweet were their songs that blessed
The marriage of Peleus and Thetis.
There was Ganymede, the darling of Zeus's bed, drawing libations of wine
From deep in the bowls of gold.
On the shining white sand the fifty daughters of Nereus
Wove the tapestry of the marriage dance.

A thunder of hooves.
Centaurs careened through the green of the
    pines.
The still air rang with their cries. "Oh daughter
    of Nereus!
Chiron, the prophet that knows the wisdom of
    Apollo, speaks.
You will bear a son to be a glorious light unto
    Thessaly.
With shield and spear he will lead the
    Myrmidons to Troy.
He will set the land of Priam aflame,
His body in armor of gold fashioned by
    Hephaestus,
A gift of Thetis, his mother."

On that day the gods blessed the marriage of
    Peleus and Thetis.

But for you, Iphigenia, there will be a different
    crown.
The curls of your hair the Greeks will adorn with
    a wreath,
Will take you like a brindled calf, pure, from a
    cave in the mountain rocks,
Will stain a human throat with blood.
You were not reared in the hills
To the sound of the shepherd's pipe or the
    herdsman's flute.
In your mother's arms were you raised
To be one day an Argive bride,
Crowned with flowers.
How can the face of Shame or Virtue save you
When Sin sits on her throne?
When Virtue's face is hidden by man,
And man pays her no mind?
When lawlessness rules and laws die,
And man does not fear the anger of the gods?

CLYTEMNESTRA: I have come out of the house. I have been waiting for Agamemnon. He has been away now for a long time. My daughter weeps. In her grief she sounds all the notes of sorrow, for she knows of the death which her father plans. Here Agamemnon comes. His guilt will soon be revealed—savage stratagems against his own daughter.

AGAMEMNON: Daughter of Leda, it is good that I find you outside. I wish to speak to you alone. The girl must not hear. A young bride should not be party to what I have to say.

CLYTEMNESTRA: So, it is good that you find me here. Why so?

AGAMEMNON: Bring her out here to me! The holy waters are prepared. The offerings of meal are ready to be purified by fire. The victims stand awaiting sacrifice before the marriage ceremony.

(a lie)

disgusting

CLYTEMNESTRA: *(aside)* You say all the right words, but what you do—ah, there are no right words for that.

Come daughter, come outside. *(at door)* You know what your father means to do. Bring your brother, wrap him in your cloak, daughter, come outside. See, she comes. She listens to her father. An obedient child. But I have things to say. I shall speak for her.

AGAMEMNON: Why are you crying? Speak to me, child. Come on, smile. Look at me. Look up. Take the cloak away from your eyes.

CLYTEMNESTRA: *(aside)* Where do I begin? Where can my grief find force? Beginning, middle, end—'tis all alike.

49

AGAMEMNON: Now what is the matter? Did you plan to show me faces filled with fear and alarm?

CLYTEMNESTRA: Answer me like a man, husband of mine.

AGAMEMNON: You can ask what you want. I am willing to answer.

CLYTEMNESTRA: Here is your daughter, my daughter— are you going to kill her?

AGAMEMNON: What a cruel thing to say! You have no right to accuse me of—

CLYTEMNESTRA: Be calm. Answer my question.

AGAMEMNON: Ask a reasonable question, you will get a reasonable answer.

CLYTEMNESTRA: I ask one question only. Answer me.

AGAMEMNON: Why me? Aaah! You cruel gods, why me?

CLYTEMNESTRA: And why me? Why her? A cruel fate for three.

AGAMEMNON: Who has done you wrong?

CLYTEMNESTRA: You ask me that? Do not try to be clever. It does not suit you.

AGAMEMNON: I am finished. My secret pain is no secret anymore.

CLYTEMNESTRA: I know everything. I know what you mean to do to me. Your silence speaks your guilt. You groan and weep. There is no need to say the words.

AGAMEMNON: Yes, I am silent now. I will not lie. Why add shame to the list of my misfortunes?

CLYTEMNESTRA: Listen to what I must say. I shall be plain. No more evasion. No more games. First, this. You took me in marriage against my will. You took me by force. You killed my husband, Tantalus. You tore my child from my arms, threw him to the ground, and kicked him to death. Castor and Pollux, my brothers and twin sons of Zeus, made war upon you on their gleaming white horses. But my father, Tyndareus, intervened on your behalf. You became his suppliant, and he gave me to you for wife. I made my peace with you, and you cannot deny that I became a wife without blame for you and your house. I was faithful to you. You came home happy, you left happy. You were a lucky man to have found such a wife. A bad wife is not hard to find. I bore you a son. A son, after three daughters. And now I am to lose a child—to a cruel death. If someone were to ask you why, tell me, what would you say? Shall I speak for you? I know why. So that Menelaus may get his wife back. Helen. A daughter for a whore! Exchange what we love for a thing of hate! Now think of me. You will go off to war, and leave me at home—you are gone for a long time. How do you think my heart will feel? I walk through empty rooms, see the chairs that once she sat on, pass by the girls' bedrooms—empty now. What will I do but sit and weep, nothing to do but weep forever?

Believe me, that is not what I want. I want you home. Your daughters want you home. Do not force me, I beg you, to forget my duty toward you. Do not forget your *own* duty. Your duty to your child. When you make the sacrifice of your daughter, what will be the words of your prayer? What blessing will you ask for as you cut her throat? Will you ask for a return home that matches

51

the shame and the pain of your departure? And
what of me? Is it right for me to pray for your success? We would have to believe that the gods are
fools if we pray for the happiness of a murderer.

When you come home to Argos, will you take
your children in your arms? God forbid. Could
they look you in the eye, hold out their arms to
be held—and feel the knife cut away their life?
Did you think of this? Or do you merely play the
king and strut like a general?

This is what you should have said to the
Greeks—*this* would have been fair and just—"Do
you want to sail to Troy, soldiers of the Greek
army? Then choose by lot whose child must die!"
Is it fair and just to offer up your own child, a single victim for all the Greeks? Why shouldn't
Menelaus sacrifice his own daughter, Hermione,
for her mother's sake? It is *his* quarrel. But it is I,
I who have been loyal to your bed, *I* must lose my
child. And she, the whore Helen, will keep her
daughter. Safe home in Sparta she will smile at
her good fortune. Answer me. Tell me if anything
I have said is untrue. If I have said the truth, find
your senses and do not kill our sweet child.

CHORUS: Oh listen to her. Change your mind. Together you can save her. No man will blame you.

IPHIGENIA: If I had the tongue of Orpheus, father, an
eloquence that could move stones and make
them trail behind me, if I could cast a spell upon
all who listened to me, I would now use my art.
But I have only this to offer—my grief. My tears
are my only art. And I weep. Like the branch of a
tree that bends to the earth, I kneel here in supplication. The body that touches you now my
mother gave to you in childbirth. It is sweet to
look up at the light of the sun. Let me not see

only the black darkness of death forever. I was your first, the first to call you father, the first that you called child, the first to lie content and safe in your arms, the first to kiss and be kissed. I remember you saying, "Sweet child, will I live to see you married—happy, full of life in another's home; a mother too, perhaps, bringing joy and respect to my family?" Then I would take you by the beard, as I do now, and I would say, "And what about you, father? When you are old, shall I greet you at the door of my house, with open arms, take you aside and pay you back in love for all the love I got from you as a child?" I remember what we said. But you have forgotten. You want to kill me. Oh no, I beg you, father, no—by Pelops, by Atreus your father, and by my mother here who gave birth to me in pain so many years ago and now suffers pain a second time. What is Paris to me? Or Helen? Their illicit passion has nothing to do with me. Why should I die because he took her away? Father! Look at me. Give me a look, a kiss. If you will not hear my pleas, let me at least take that memory with me to the grave.

Dear brother, you are too young to help me. But weep, my baby, weep with me. Let your tears beg your father that your sister may not die. *(Orestes cries)* Even a baby can understand another's grief. He cannot speak. But father, he begs you for mercy. Pity me, father. Have mercy for one so young. By your beard, we beg you, a baby and a young woman, we beg you, we who love you so much. A final word, my father, and one to which there is no answer. ~~It is life's sweetest gift for mortal men to look upon the light. Below, all is nothingness. A man who prays for death is mad. A simple life is better than a great death.~~

53

CHORUS: Oh hateful Helen. It is because of you and your lust that this great suffering has come upon the House of Atreus.

AGAMEMNON: I know what it is to feel pity. I love my children. I am not mad. For me to do this thing is unbearable anguish. Unbearable anguish for me not to do it: I am damned whichever I choose. Look before you, there, look upon this huge fleet of ships, this vast mass of soldiers. For the Greeks there will be no Troy. Unless, as the prophet Calchas says, I make you my sacrifice. The towers of Ilium else will stand. In the heart of the Greek army there burns a passion to sail to Troy and put an end forever to the barbarian rape of Greek wives. If I disobey the gods' command, these men will go to Argos and kill my daughters. They will kill you. They will kill me. My child, I am not the slave of Menelaus. I do not do this merely to satisfy him. No. It is for Greece that I must offer you in sacrifice—whether I will or no. For Greece must be free—as free as you and I can make her. We are Greeks. We must not allow barbarians to violate our women and carry them away from freedom. *(exit)* **ironic**

reason of her sacrifice

[The following is a duet—that is, originally it was sung, an aria of grief.]

CLYTEMNESTRA: Women, pity me. My child, I weep for your death. Your father has run away and left you to die.

light=living

IPHIGENIA: Yes, pity me, my mother, let us share the grief that lies heavy on us both. The light is dying. The sun no longer shines for me. Alas. Alas. Upon Mount Ida, in the drifting snow, in an icy cleft among the rocks, Priam abandoned the infant Paris, torn from his mother's arms. He was

called the child of Ida when he came home to
Troy. Son of the mountain, was he called. Oh how
I wish that he had died upon that mountain, not
found a herdsman's home amidst the shining
waters of the nymphs, amidst the fields that lie
thick with flowers, thick with hyacinths and roses
for the goddesses to pluck. And once among the
roses Athena came and Aphrodite, all cunning,
yes, and Hera. Hermes, messenger of Zeus,
watched. Aphrodite was proud of the passion she
inspired, Athena of the spear, Hera of her marriage to Zeus the king. And so—the judgment fell
to Paris, hateful judgment—for them a prize of
beauty, for me a prize of death. But for the
Greeks, oh women, now comes glory, for Artemis
accepts the sacrifice., And they will sail to Troy.
But my father, he that made me, mother, oh my
mother, he has gone and left me. I curse the day
when first I set eyes upon Helen, evil Helen. For
her I die. Killed, butchered by a father who has
forgotten god. I curse this place—Aulis, that took
within her harbors the ships with prows of
bronze, the ships that carry men to Troy. Why did
Zeus stop the winds upon Euripus? *We* could not
sail. But to other men he sends the winds and
they rejoice and sail upon the sea. He fills their
sails or lets them fall and rest. Men are born to
sorrow. Their life is but a day, and they are born
to sorrow. The end of life is suffering and now,
alas, the suffering is great. Great the pain that
Helen brings upon the Greeks.

CHORUS: I pity you. You are suffering a sorrow that
was not yours to bear.

IPHIGENIA: Mother, I see a crowd of men approach-
ing.

CLYTEMNESTRA: It is Achilles, my child—he to whom you were promised.

IPHIGENIA: Servants, open the doors. I must hide myself.

CLYTEMNESTRA: Why do you run away, child?

IPHIGENIA: I am ashamed to look upon Achilles.

CLYTEMNESTRA: Why?

IPHIGENIA: I am ashamed of this marriage, this unhappy marriage.

CLYTEMNESTRA: This is not the time for modesty. Stay here. Listen to me. We may be able to help ourselves.

(enter Achilles)

ACHILLES: Daughter of Leda, unhappy lady—

CLYTEMNESTRA: You speak the truth.

ACHILLES: The Greeks are up in arms. They are shouting that—

CLYTEMNESTRA: What is it about? Tell me.

ACHILLES: About your child. They say—

CLYTEMNESTRA: I can sense the worst.

ACHILLES: They say that she must die.

CLYTEMNESTRA: And does no one take her part?

ACHILLES: I found myself in some danger.

CLYTEMNESTRA: What danger?

ACHILLES: They began to stone me.

CLYTEMNESTRA: For speaking for my daughter?

ACHILLES: Yes.

CLYTEMNESTRA: Who had the arrogance to lay hands on you?

ACHILLES: All of them.

CLYTEMNESTRA: And what about your own men, the Myrmidons?

ACHILLES: They were the first to attack me.

CLYTEMNESTRA: My child, this is the end.

ACHILLES: They turned on me, called me a woman-izer.

CLYTEMNESTRA: And what did you say?

ACHILLES: That they had no right to kill the woman who was to be my wife . . .

CLYTEMNESTRA: That was right.

ACHILLES: When her father had promised her to me . . .

CLYTEMNESTRA: He even sent for her from Argos.

ACHILLES: But I was shouted down.

CLYTEMNESTRA: There is nothing more terrifying than a mob.

ACHILLES: I am here to protect you.

CLYTEMNESTRA: You cannot fight against that crowd of men single-handedly.

ACHILLES: You see my guards here?

CLYTEMNESTRA: May the gods reward your courage.

ACHILLES: A reward shall be mine.

CLYTEMNESTRA: Then my child will not be killed?

ACHILLES: Never. I will not allow it.

CLYTEMNESTRA: Do they plan to take her by force?

ACHILLES: Yes. A mob is gathering, Odysseus at the head.

CLYTEMNESTRA: Ah, the seed of Sisyphus?

ACHILLES: No less.

CLYTEMNESTRA: Is this his own idea or did the army force it upon him?

ACHILLES: He was chosen—a willing servant.

CLYTEMNESTRA: A wicked choice—to commit murder.

ACHILLES: I shall stop him.

CLYTEMNESTRA: Will he seize her, drag her off, even if she resists?

ACHILLES: Of course he will—by her golden hair.

CLYTEMNESTRA: What must I do?

ACHILLES: Hold on to your daughter.

CLYTEMNESTRA: If that is all, she shall not die.

ACHILLES: It will come to that.

IPHIGENIA: Mother, hear what I have to say—and you, sir. You are angry with your husband. Anger will have no effect. It is impossible for him to take a stand when the odds against him are so high. *detachment* This man deserves our praise, our thanks for his *agamemnon* courage. But we must not let his reputation in the army be destroyed. We would still suffer what we are to suffer, and he would pay a terrible price. Mother, as I stood here I have been thinking, and I have come to a conclusion. I have decided that I must die. And I shall die gloriously. I have been able to wash all thoughts of bitterness from my mind. Mother, I want you to look at all this with

ultimate sacrifice

58

*for a cause—
a martyr*

me, join me, see that I am right. The entire Greek
army is dependent on me. On me depends the
passage of ships across the sea, and on me depends the death of Troy. Only thus will barbarians never again steal Greek women from their
homes. My death shall bring these things to pass.
I shall be known as the woman who set Greece
free. And I shall be blessed. It is not right for me
to love life too much.

You brought me up not for yourself alone but
for the greater good of all the Greeks. Ten thousand men stand, shield in hand. Ten thousand
men wait to dip their oars in the sea. Their country has been wronged, and these brave men will
fight a glorious fight and are prepared to die for
Greece. Shall my simple life make this impossible? Where then lies justice? There is no answer
to the question. I have one more point to make.
It is not right that this man take up arms alone
against his friends and die for me, a woman. A
man's life is worth more than ten thousand
women. Artemis has determined to take this my
body—can I, a mere mortal, thwart a goddess's
will? It cannot be. I give my life for Greece. Sacrifice me and destroy Troy. That will be my epitaph
for eternity. That will be my glory, my marriage,
my children. Greeks must rule barbarians. That is
nature's law, mother. Barbarians must not rule
over Greeks. For they are slaves, Greeks are free.

*meaning
of her
life*

CHORUS: Young woman, you are noble and brave.
Fate and the goddess are to blame.

ACHILLES: Daughter of Agamemnon, if I could win
you for my wife, I would know that some god had
smiled upon me. Because of you Greece is
blessed and you blessed in Greece. You breathed
noble words, and your country was honored by

them. The gods are stronger than you, and you surrendered to their will. You looked necessity in the face and saw your duty. When I think upon your nobility, I long more deeply for your love. For you *are* noble. Listen to me. I have a deep desire to help you, a deep desire to take you with me to my home. If I do not face the Greeks, I swear by my mother, Thetis, the sorrow will be mine. I must save your life. Think, my child, death is a fearful thing.

IPHIGENIA: I speak to you plain truth. Helen, because of her beauty, has caused quarrels enough, enough death amongst men. You do not know me. Do not die for me. And do not kill for me. Let me, if I can, make Greece free.

ACHILLES: Yours is a noble soul. I have no more to say, if that is your decision. A noble soul—I speak the truth. And yet, if you have a change of heart, I shall be ready—I shall go to the altar, lay my weapons near, and be ready to stand and save you from death. Perhaps, perhaps when the cruel knife is laid against your throat you will call on me. No, I will not let you die impulsively, unthinking. I go to the temple of Artemis. With these weapons in my hand I shall await your coming. *(exit)*

IPHIGENIA: Mother, do not fill your eyes with tears. Why weep? Speak to me.

CLYTEMNESTRA: Why? Oh ask me not the reason why. My heart breaks.

IPHIGENIA: Speak no more. You will make a coward of me. Help me now.

CLYTEMNESTRA: Tell me how. I will always do you right.

IPHIGENIA: Then do not cut your hair in mourning. Do not cover your body in robes of black.

CLYTEMNESTRA: Why do you ask this of me? For I have lost my child.

IPHIGENIA: ~~You have not lost me. I am saved. And you will be made glorious by my death.~~

CLYTEMNESTRA: Why do you say this? May I not mourn for your death?

IPHIGENIA: No, you must not mourn. No tomb will be laid for me.

CLYTEMNESTRA: We mourn for the dead, not for their monuments.

IPHIGENIA: My headstone will be the altar of Artemis.

CLYTEMNESTRA: My child, I will do as you ask. I understand.

IPHIGENIA: I am blessed. I am to be the savior of Greece.

CLYTEMNESTRA: Do you have a message for your sisters?

IPHIGENIA: Let them not mourn in robes of black.

CLYTEMNESTRA: Some last words of love for them?

IPHIGENIA: Tell them farewell. And for Orestes here, raise him to be a man.

CLYTEMNESTRA: Hold him in your arms one last time.

IPHIGENIA: Sweet child, you did all you could to help your sister.

CLYTEMNESTRA: And in Argos—what can I do for you there?

61

IPHIGENIA: Do not hate the man you married, my father.

CLYTEMNESTRA: His life must be lived in fear because of you.

IPHIGENIA: This was not his wish. He put an end to me that Greece might live.

CLYTEMNESTRA: Yes, by treachery and cowardice—he is not fit to bear his father's name.

IPHIGENIA: I do not wish to be dragged to the altar by my hair. Who will take me there?

CLYTEMNESTRA: I will go with you—

IPHIGENIA: No. That would not be right.

CLYTEMNESTRA: Oh dear god, I shall cling to you, hold you.

IPHIGENIA: No, mother, no. You must stay behind. It will be easier for me and for you. Let one of my father's men take me to the field of Artemis where I must die.

CLYTEMNESTRA: My child, do not leave me.

IPHIGENIA: I must. Never to return.

CLYTEMNESTRA: Do not leave your mother.

IPHIGENIA: I must. My heart is strong.

CLYTEMNESTRA: No! Stay. Stay with me.

IPHIGENIA: You must not weep. I forbid it. *(to the Chorus)* Let a hymn of praise be sung. May the omens be good. Sing to Artemis, daughter of Zeus. In the Greek camp let there be holy silence. Now the sacred rites begin, baskets of flowers in the offering fire. And my father will circle the altar, slow of foot, from left to right. I bring to Greece salvation and victory.

[Monody, originally sung] Lead me on, for I am a sacker of cities, destroyer of Troy. Give me garlands, crown my hair, wash me in streams of holy water and dance about the temple, dance about the altar of Artemis, Artemis the blessed goddess queen. With my blood, with my sacrifice, I shall wash clean the words of her command. That is her will. Mother, mother that I love. I must not weep for you. In the holy place of death, tears must not flow. Women, join me now, sing with me in praise of Artemis. Here is she worshiped, here in Aulis where in the narrows and the harbors the ships lie still and the spear men in their anger thirst to fight, thirst for blood. And all for me. I call upon the land of Greece, my home—I call upon Mycenae.

CHORUS: Your home—where Perseus raised the walls and the Cyclops labored long.

IPHIGENIA: You raised me to be a flame that shines on Greece. I am not afraid to die.

CLYTEMNESTRA: You will know everlasting fame.

IPHIGENIA: I call upon the Light of Day, upon the radiant face of Zeus. I go now to another life and to another world. Sweet light of day I bid you farewell. *(exeunt Clytemnestra and Iphigenia)*

CHORUS: Look upon her, the sacker of cities, destroyer of Troy. Give her garlands, crown her hair, wash her in streams of holy water. Look upon her as she goes to stain the altar of the goddess with flowing streams of blood, blood streaming from her throat, her soft and lovely throat. Your father waits.

The holy water is ready to be sprinkled.
The sacred bowls are ready and the army waits,
 ready to sail to Troy.
But we must sing in praise of Artemis, child of
 Zeus, queen amongst the gods.
We pray for a fate that brings success.
Lady, holy queen, let your anger be silenced by
 the death of this child.
Free the army of the Greeks. Let them sail upon
 the flowing streams of the sea to the land of
 Troy, where treachery finds its home.
Set Agamemnon free.
Let him crown the spears of the Greeks with a
 wreath of fame.
Crown his brows with a wreath of glory that will
 not die.

[The rest of the play as it stands is deeply suspect.
An ancient quote mentions Artemis as appearing
and saying to Clytemnestra, "I shall place before
the Greeks a horned deer. And as they raise their
hands in sacrifice they will believe it is your
daughter." This would be very Euripidean—to
have a *deus ex machina* at this point. What we *have*
is the appearance of a messenger, who recounts
the substitution and the sacrifice.]

MESSENGER: Clytemnestra! Daughter of Tyndareus,
 come outside. Hear what I have to say.

CLYTEMNESTRA: I hear you and I come. I am in pain
 with shock, distracted by fear. Can you be bringing me news more painful than before?

MESSENGER: I have wonderful yet frightening news to
 tell you of your child.

CLYTEMNESTRA: Then speak. Quickly tell me all there
 is to know.

64

MESSENGER: Yes, my queen, you shall learn of it. I shall begin at the beginning and tell you everything—unless my mind begins to falter and my tongue fails me as I speak. When we arrived at the field of Artemis, daughter of Zeus, the field that is filled with flowers, we brought your child to the place where the Greek army had gathered, all together and all at once. When King Agamemnon saw his daughter proceeding to the altar to her death, he heaved a deep sigh and turned his head to one side and wept. He covered his eyes with his robe. But the young girl stood beside her father who had given her life and said: "Father, as you bid me, I am here. I give my body, freely on behalf of my country, for all the land of Greece. Lead me to the altar. There, if that is the gods' will, sacrifice me. May this gift from me bring you success. May you win the crown of victory and win thereafter a glorious homecoming. And no, do not let any man lay his hands upon me. In peace and in good heart I offer you my throat."

So she spoke, and all stood by in wonder at the courage, yes, the virtue of her words. Then Talthybius, for so he was commanded, stood before the assembled army and ordered them to watch and keep holy silence. Then Calchas, the prophet, took from its sheath a sharp knife and put it in a basket studded with gold. And upon the young girl's head he put a garland.

Achilles, son of Peleus, circled the altar of the goddess, basket in hand, and upon her he sprinkled holy water and he said, "Artemis, daughter of Zeus, slayer of wild beasts, you that spin the silver light at night, receive this sacrifice which we offer to you. We the Greek army and King Agamemnon offer to you the pure blood that flows from a virgin's throat. Grant our ships an untroubled journey. Grant that our spears will sack the towers of Troy." The priest seized the knife and offered a prayer as he looked for a place to plunge the knife's point. My soul was deeply troubled and in pain. I stood by, head lowered.

Suddenly, it was a miracle: everyone had heard the sound of the knife—but no one could see where in the world the young maid had disappeared to. The priest cried out. The army echoed his cry. And then they saw the miracle, impossible to believe even as it happened before their eyes. There on the ground lay a deer, gasping for breath. She was a full-grown deer, beautiful, and the altar of the goddess was dripping with her blood. Then Calchas spoke—imagine the joy!— "Leaders of this the Greek army, do you see this victim that the goddess has laid upon her own altar? This mountain deer? She accepts this offering with greater gladness than the child. For her altar will not now be stained with noble blood. She rejoices in the sacrifice. And she grants us fair sailing and success at Troy. Therefore, courage! To arms, to the ships! For on this day we must leave the hollow bay of Aulis and cross the Aegean Sea." When the carcass had been reduced to ashes in Hephaestus's fire, Calchas offered a prayer for the safe homecoming of the army.

Agamemnon sent me to tell you these things, to tell you of the good fortune he has received from the gods, and of the fame that is now his and will not die. I tell you what I saw. For I was there. There is no doubt your child has been taken to live amongst the gods. Put aside your grief and your anger against your husband. Mortals cannot understand the will of the gods. But they save those they love. Your child, this day, saw death and life.

CHORUS: I rejoice to hear your words. He tells you that your child lives and is amongst the gods.

CLYTEMNESTRA: My child, my child, what god has stolen you? How shall I call upon you? What am I to say? Is this only an idle story meant to comfort me, to staunch my grief for you?

CHORUS: Here comes King Agamemnon. He will tell you the same story.

AGAMEMNON: Lady, we can be happy for our daughter, for she is truly at one with the gods. You must now leave for home and take with you this young prince, Orestes. The army waits, ready to sail. Farewell. It will be long before I speak to you again. After Troy. May all be well with you.

CHORUS: Go in joy, son of Atreus, go to the land of Troy and return in joy. May all the gods will it, return laden with the spoils of war.

ELEPHANT PAPERBACKS

Theatre and Drama
Robert Brustein, *Dumbocracy in America,* EL421
Robert Brustein, *Reimagining American Theatre,* EL410
Robert Brustein, *The Theatre of Revolt,* EL407
Stephen Citron, *The Musical from the Inside Out,* EL427
Irina and Igor Levin, *Working on the Play and the Role,* EL411
Plays for Performance:
    Aristophanes, *Lysistrata,* EL405
    Pierre Augustin de Beaumarchais, *The Marriage of Figaro,* EL418
    Anton Chekhov, *The Cherry Orchard,* EL420
    Anton Chekhov, *The Seagull,* EL407
    Euripides, *The Bacchae,* EL419
    Euripides, *Iphigenia in Aulis,* EL423
    Euripides, *Iphigenia Among the Taurians,* EL424
    Georges Feydeau, *Paradise Hotel,* EL403
    Henrik Ibsen, *Ghosts,* EL401
    Henrik Ibsen, *Hedda Gabler,* EL413
    Henrik Ibsen, *The Master Builder,* EL417
    Henrik Ibsen, *When We Dead Awaken,* EL408
    Henrik Ibsen, *The Wild Duck,* EL425
    Heinrich von Kleist, *The Prince of Homburg,* EL402
    Christopher Marlowe, *Doctor Faustus,* EL404
    The Mysteries: Creation, EL412
    The Mysteries: The Passion, EL414
    Luigi Pirandello, *Six Characters in Search of an Author,* EL426
    Sophocles, *Electra,* EL415
    August Strindberg, *The Father,* EL406
    August Strindberg, *Miss Julie,* EL422